MALAYSIA

A TRUE BOOK®

by

Ann Heinrichs

Children's Press®

A Division of Scholastic Inc.

New York Toronto London Auckland Sydney
Mexico City New Delhi Hong Kong
Danbury, Connecticut

A village on stilts in Mabul

Content Consultant
Dr. Amy J. Johnson, Ph.D.
Berry College

Reading Consultant
Sonja I. Smith
Reading Specialist

Library of Congress Cataloging-in-Publication Data

Heinrichs, Ann.
    Malaysia / Ann Heinrichs.
        p. cm. — (A true book)
Includes bibliographical references and index.
Contents: Mountains, forests, and coasts—One land, many cultures—
Kingdoms, traders, and a modern nation—Farms, factories, and mines—
Daily life and celebrations.
    ISBN 0-516-22812-9 (lib. bdg.)   0-516-26957-7 (pbk.)
    1. Malaysia—Juvenile literature. [1. Malaysia.] I. Title. II. Series.
DS592.H4 2004
959.5—dc22

2003018665

Contents

THAILAND

MALAYSIA

South
China
Sea

PENINSULAR
MAL

Ipoh

⭐ Kuala Lumpur

Johor Bah

Strait of Malacca

SUMATRA

SINGA

Sandakan

ABAH

Gomantong
Caves

I N D   E S I A

INDIAN
OCEAN

N
W   E
S

0   400 miles

0   600 kilometers

MALAYSIA

Mountains, Forests, and Coasts

Malaysia is a country in Southeast Asia. It is made up of two separate regions. One is called East Malaysia. The other is Peninsular Malaysia. Between these two regions is the South China Sea.

East Malaysia covers the northwestern part of the island of

A scenic view of Sandakan,
on the east coast of Sabah.

Borneo. It is divided into two states—Sarawak and Sabah. Along the coast is the tiny nation of Brunei. The rest of this island belongs to Indonesia.

Peninsular Malaysia is located on the Malay **Peninsula**. The Malay Peninsula extends south of Thailand. Peninsular Malaysia is divided into eleven states.

Many mountain ranges run down the peninsula from north to south. The mountains slope toward lowlands along the coasts. The west coast is the most developed region. Kuala Lumpur, the capital and largest city, lies on the west coast.

High mountains separate East Malaysia from neighboring

The mountainous countryside of Malaysia

Indonesia. Mount Kinabalu towers high above them all. It is Malaysia's highest peak. Low plains line East Malaysia's coast. Between the mountains and the plains are steep hills and narrow valleys. Many rivers and streams rush down the mountainsides.

Malaysia's Caves

Deer Cave in Mulu National Park

Malaysia has some of the world's biggest caves. They were formed over millions of years as underground rivers wore away the soft limestone. Gomantong Caves in Sabah are known for their birds' nests, which are prized as a food. Local people climb bamboo ladders to collect the nests. Sarawak's Mulu National Park contains many caves with massive chambers and miles-long passageways.

Dark Cave is in Batu Caves near Kuala Lumpur. Glistening, multicolored rock formations hang down from the ceiling and rise up from the floor. Bats, frogs, snakes, and other cave-dwelling animals live there.

Dense **rain forests** cover much of Malaysia. Their tall evergreen trees have thick, leathery leaves. Thousands of plant and animal species live in these forests.

Malaysia's forests are home to elephants, tigers, wild pigs, and rhinoceroses. Proboscis monkeys live in East Malaysia. They have long noses and long tails. Orangutans live in East Malaysia, too. These large apes have been disappearing because of hunting. They are now protected by law.

Malaysia's rain forests (top) attract visitors from all over the world. Orangutans (above) and proboscis monkeys (left) live there.

Malaysia Through History

People have lived in Malaysia for thousands of years. Malays began settling on the Malay Peninsula around 1000 B.C. They were a mixture of many peoples from Southeast Asia, India, and China.

Around 100 B.C., explorers from India arrived in Kedah, in

the northwest corner of Peninsular Malaysia. Over the next several centuries, Indian traders established bases in Kedah. They traded the region's gold, wood, and spices. The Indians established kingdoms and spread Indian culture throughout the land. Two of India's religions, Hinduism and Buddhism, took hold.

Paramesvara, a Sumatran prince, founded the kingdom of Malacca around A.D.1400.

Malacca overlooks the **Strait** of Malacca. This waterway was the main sea route between India and China. Traders from many lands stopped in Malacca. Among them were Arab traders who introduced the religion of Islam. Paramesvara himself converted to the new religion, and it spread throughout Malacca and neighboring regions.

Malacca's rulers—including Paramesvara—began calling themselves **sultans**. Under the

The Bujang Valley

Ancient temples and shrines have been found in the Bujang Valley.

Malaysia's richest ancient site lies in Kedah's Bujang Valley. It contains the ruins of Hindu and Buddhist kingdoms that existed from the A.D. 400s to 1300s. More than fifty temples have been found there. A museum built in the valley preserves tools, ornaments, and religious objects found in the area. By studying these objects, researchers are learning about the ancient kingdoms' **cultures** and values.

sultans, Malacca became the leading trade center in Southeast Asia. This period is known as the Golden Age of Malacca. The Golden Age came to an end when the Portuguese took over Malacca in 1511. The Dutch captured Malacca in 1641. Next, the British took control.

In 1867, Great Britain established the Straits Settlements. This **colony** included Malacca, Singapore, and Penang Island.

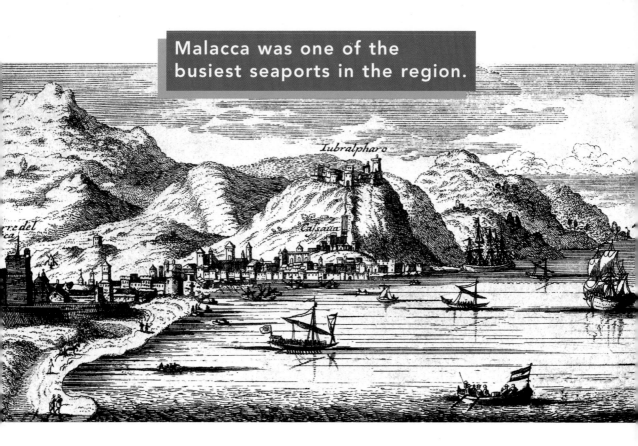
Malacca was one of the busiest seaports in the region.

Sarawak and Sabah, on the island of Borneo, gradually came under British control, too. In the 1940s, Malaysians began to push for freedom from Britain. Independence came at

Malaysian soldiers salute the flag during a celebration of their country's independence in 1957.

last in 1957. The new Federation of Malaysia was formed in 1963. Its thirteen states included Sarawak and Sabah. Singapore became a separate republic in 1965.

Today, Malaysia's government is a constitutional monarchy. The nation has a king, or sultan, and a constitution outlining its basic ruling principles. The supreme head of the federation is the head of state. He is a sultan whose main role is to preside over official ceremonies.

The sultan of Pahang (right) presides over an official ceremony.

The parliament in action

The parliament is Malaysia's lawmaking body. It consists of a senate and a house of represen-tatives. The sultan appoints the prime minister, who is the head of Malaysia's government.

One Land, Many Cultures

Malaysia is home to many **ethnic** groups. They give the country a rich mix of cultures, languages, and religions. Malaysia's different cultures are very open to one another. For example, members of any faith are welcome to take part in the many religious festivals that take place throughout the year.

21

A group of Malaysian children ride on a rickshaw.

About 24 million people live in Malaysia. Four out of every five Malaysians live on Peninsular Malaysia. Malays are the country's largest ethnic group. They make up about half the population. Malays speak

Malay, officially called Bahasa Melayu, Malaysia's national language. Almost all Malays are Muslims, or members of the religion of Islam.

Chinese people are the next-largest ethnic group.

Malaysian Muslims participate in morning prayers.

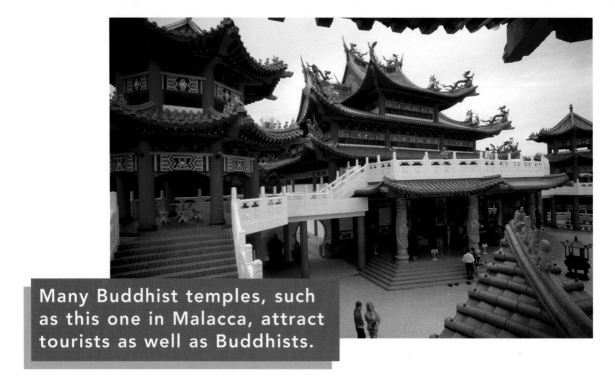

Many Buddhist temples, such as this one in Malacca, attract tourists as well as Buddhists.

Many Chinese people practice the religion of Buddhism. Others follow Taoism, which is partly a religion and partly a way of thinking. Taoism teaches people to follow a peaceful, simple, and orderly way of life.

South Asian peoples also settled on Peninsular Malaysia. Tamils originated in Sri Lanka, an island off the coast of India. People from India and Pakistan live on the peninsula, too.

The Orang Asli are the original settlers of Peninsular Malaysia. They have lived there for at least five thousand years. These tribal people are made up of several ethnic and language groups.

Most still pursue their **traditional** ways of life—hunting, fishing, and gathering plants—while others are

Many of the Orang Asli depend on the forest for food and other resources.

farmers. The Orang Asli follow an ancient animist religion. This means that they honor the spirits of animals, plants, and the forces of nature.

East Malaysia has even more ethnic variety. In Sabah, the Kadazan are the major group.

They are organized into tribes. In Sarawak, the Chinese and the Iban are the largest groups. Other ethnic groups in Malaysia include people from Europe, America, Australia, Thailand, and the Middle East.

Iban women weave colorful mats.

Farms, Factories, and Mines

Manufacturing is Malaysia's biggest industry. Malaysia is a top producer of computer parts and other electronics. Some factories make cloth, foods, and cars. Others take local products and process them into goods for sale.

Workers build cars at a plant in Pegoh.

People have mined tin in Malaysia for hundreds of years. The country's tin supplies are among the largest in the world.

However, petroleum and natural gas are Malaysia's most valuable mining products.

Many farmers in Malaysia grow rice. Some also grow pineapples, bananas, mangoes, coffee, and coconuts. Malaysia's cacao beans are made into chocolate. Black pepper is an important crop in Sarawak.

Malaysia is the world's largest **exporter** of palm oil. This oil is made from palm-tree nuts. It is used in cooking and in making

Harvesting rice (left) and cacao beans (below)

A man extracts the milky liquid called latex from the trunk of a rubber tree.

soap. Malaysia is also a leading

source of rubber. It is made

from ... of the

I can infer
thet he is hard
working.

rubber tree. Workers make cuts in the bark to tap, or collect, the latex.

Malaysia's forests contain valuable wood, which is used to make furniture. Unfortunately, logging has destroyed much of Malaysia's forestland. As the forests are cleared, many tribal people lose their homelands. Dozens of animal species also lose their homes and die out. Some areas in Malaysia have been set aside as national parks.

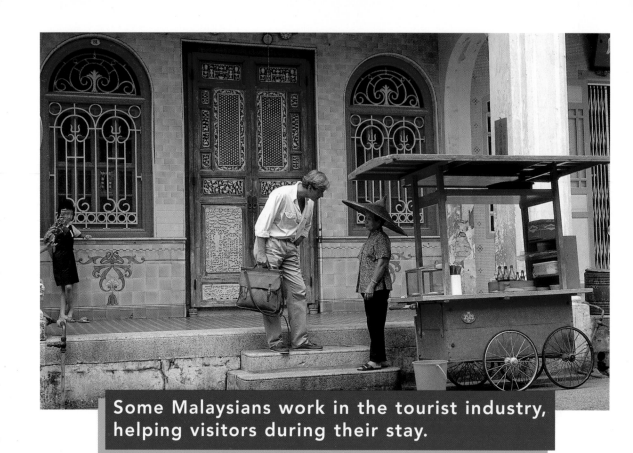

Some Malaysians work in the tourist industry, helping visitors during their stay.

Tourism is a growing industry in Malaysia. Many visitors explore its rain forests, caves, national parks, and ancient sites. Others enjoy meeting local people.

Daily Life and Celebrations

More than half of all Malaysians live in cities and towns. Most city people live in apartment buildings. Kuala Lumpur, the capital, is a busy, modern city. Its Petronas Towers are among the tallest buildings in the world.

Life is very different outside cities and towns. Villages in

The Petronas Towers in Kuala Lumpur (left); Traditional kampong houses (below).

Peninsular Malaysia are called *kampongs*. Kampong houses are made of wood and built on stilts. This keeps them safe from floodwaters.

In Sabah and Sarawak, most villages are located along rivers. Villagers hunt, fish, and plant small fields of crops. They travel in long wooden boats called *perahus*.

Most Malaysians dress as Europeans or Americans do. Many Muslim women wear long skirts and head scarves. On special occasions, people from each ethnic

Muslim women dress modestly in public, often wearing long skirts and head scarves.

group wear traditional clothes. For Malays, the traditional outfit is a loose shirt and batik skirt. Batik is cloth th_____lorful pattern_____the traditio_____

Mala_____red from lo_____art of

most meals. It is served with vegetables, fish, or meat. Muslims, however, do not eat pork or drink alcohol, which are forbidden by Islamic law.

Malaysians perform many traditional dances. The dancers

Malaysian dancers perform the Sumazau, the national dance of Sabah.

wear elaborate costumes and tell stories with movements. For tribal people, many dances and ceremonies are based on ancient beliefs and tales.

Sepak takraw is a popular Malaysian sport. It is similar to volleyball and soccer. Malaysian martial arts, or fighting styles, are called *silat*. Other traditional sports are top-spinning (*gasing*) and flying giant kites (*wau*).

Festivals in Malaysia reflect its many cultures. *Hari Raya*

Sepak takraw is one of the most popular sports in Asia.

Aidilfitri is a major Muslim feast. It marks the end of Ramadan, the Islamic month of fasting. People gather for prayers, visit loved ones' graves, and enjoy festive meals. In Sabah, the

Kadazans celebrate *Kaamatan* after the harvest.

Chinese New Year is an important Chinese holiday. So is the Mooncake Festival. It celebrates autumn's full moon. Indians celebrate *Deepavali*, the

Hindu Festival of Lights. They adorn their homes with dozens of lights. This represents the victory of good over evil.

Malaysia is truly a land of many cultures. Yet Malaysians respect one another's customs while keeping their special traditions alive.

An Indian boy lights dozens of lamps during the Festival of Lights.

To Find Out More

Here are some additional resources to help you learn more about Malaysia.

 **Books**

Department of Geography, Lerner Publications. **Malaysia in Pictures.** Lerner, 1997.

Goodman, Susan, and Michael Doolittle (photographer). **Chopsticks for My Noodle Soup: Eliza's Life in Malaysia.** Millbrook, 1999.

National Wildlife Federation and Sandra Stotksy. **Rain Forests: Tropical Treasures.** Chelsea House, 1998.

Rowell, Jonathan. **Malaysia.** Raintree/Steck Vaughn, 1997.

Organizations and Online Sites

Malaysian Tourism Promotion Board
120 East 56th Street, Suite 810
New York, NY 10022
212-754-1113
http://www.tourism.gov.my/

Malaysia
http://www.geographia. com/malaysia

To explore Malaysia's people, culture, history, and interesting places.

Virtual Malaysia
http://www.virtualmalaysia. com

To learn about Malaysia's arts, culture, festivals, sports, and much more.

World Wildlife Federation: Malaysia
http://www.wwfmalaysia.org

For fascinating information about Malaysia's animals, plants, rain forests, and caves.

Important Words

colony a region ruled by another country

cultures various people's customs and ways of life

ethnic relating to a race or nationality

exporter a nation that sells goods or services to another country

peninsula an area of land that is almost completely surrounded by water

rain forests dense, tropical forests that receive heavy rainfall

strait a narrow waterway

sultans Muslim kings or emperors

traditional following long-held customs

Index

Meet the Author

Ann Heinrichs grew up in Arkansas and lives in Chicago, Illinois. She has written more than one hundred books about American, European, Asian, and African history and culture. Several of her books have won national and regional awards.

Besides the United States, she has traveled in Europe, Africa, the Middle East, and East Asia. The desert is her favorite terrain.

Heinrichs holds bachelor's and master's degrees in piano performance. She practices tai chi empty-hand and sword forms and has won many awards in martial arts competitions.